INTRODUCTION

The new **self-teaching** method that allows a child to play **instantly** favorite tunes on the piano, organ or any keyboard instrument ... develops a positive self-image, due to fun and **instant** success.

All a child needs to know:

*   To recognize the letters A through G.
*   To recognize the colors black, orange and brown.
*   To recognize the sounds of favorite tunes.

Tested and evaluated by Montessori, Pre-School, Primary and Special Education classes and endorsed by **all** the teachers who tried it.

Contains Teaching Suggestions at the bottom of each song for Teachers, Day Care Centers, Camps or people in a leadership position with children.

PIANO FUN BOOK TWO TAKES YOU FURTHER INTO SHARPS, FLATS, FINGERING, CHORDS, and READING OF MUSICAL NOTES. (Available at stores carrying this book.)

D1710163

Z2711

i

DOs AND DON'Ts FOR KEYBOARD FUN

DO: *PLAY THE ORANGE AND BROWN-LETTERED NOTES WITH YOUR **RIGHT** HAND.......
              PLAY BLACK-LETTERED NOTES WITH YOUR **LEFT** HAND.

              *USE THE FINGER THAT IS MOST COMFORTABLE FOR YOU.

              *PLAY EACH SONG USING THE RHYTHM **YOU** REMEMBER. THIS IS ONE OF THE GREATEST STRENGTHS OF THIS
              TEACHING METHOD...THE RHYTHM IS BUILT-IN.

              *HAVE FUN WHILE LEARNING AND PLAYING!

DON'T: *WORRY IF YOU MAKE MISTAKES AT FIRST.....THIS IS HOW **EVERYONE** LEARNS TO PLAY THE PIANO OR ORGAN.

TO GET YOUR PIANO READY

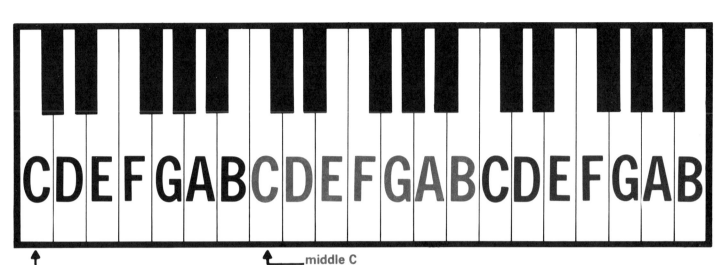

↑
17th White Key On Piano (from left to right)

↑____middle C

PLACE TABS ON WHITE KEYS FIRST:

1. Going from left to right on your piano, count up 17 white keys. (This is on a standard piano.)

*For Organs and other keyboard instruments, find Middle C and follow above example.

2. On the 17th white key, place the black lettered tabs starting with the black "C" then the black "D" and so on as shown above.

3. After you have put on the last black "B" tab, then start with the Orange "C" and place the Orange lettered tabs on through the Orange "B" as shown above.

4. After you place the last Orange "B" tab on, follow with the Brown "C" through the Brown "B".

It will help as you proceed with this book if you will memorize this order - CDEFGABC. This is called an "Octave" (8 consecutive notes).

Double check to see that your keyboard looks exactly like the picture above. (Between E and F and between B and C, make sure there are no black keys.)

TABLE OF CONTENTS

Z271151

Instant Piano Fun

Book One

by
Nancy M. Poffenberger

A Simple, Self-Teaching Method

DEDICATION

To my husband, **John,** whose constant moral support and professional advise were instrumental in the publishing of "Piano Fun."

To my three children, **Dwight, Bill** and **Molly,** who were my constant "testers" and "helpers" throughout the project.

To **Rosemary Chaney,** whose professional advise and encouragement meant so much to me.

To my obstetrician, **Dr. John Fleming,** who was most firm about my staying in bed after surgery. Were it not for "that week" I'd probably still be discussing "the book I want to write."

To my aunt, **Judy Staats,** whose enthusiasm for life and encouragement to complete "Piano Fun" was very meaningful to me.

AMERICA

Remember — For all songs, play all orange and brown lettered notes with your right hand; all black lettered with your left.

C C   D B C   D

MY   COUN.....TRY   'TIS   OF   THEE

E   E   FE   DC   DCBC

SWEET   LAND   OF   LI.....BER.....TY ⁻   OF   THEE   I   SING

G   G   GG   F E

LAND   WHERE   MY   FA.....THER   DIED

F   FF   F   E   D

LAND   OF   THE   PIL.....GRIM'S   PRIDE

EFEDC   E   FG

FROM   EV.....ER.....Y   MOUN.....TAIN.....SIDE

AF   E   DC

LE....T   FREE.....DOM   RING.

TEACHING SUGGESTIONS:

Remind the children this is a patriotic hymn of the United States written by Samuel Francis Smith. He was studying to be a minister when he wrote the song in 1832.

(The above information would be of interest to the 2nd and 3rd grades only. With the other ages, I would just sing and enjoy it without discussing patriotism.)

MARY HAD A LITTLE LAMB

E D C D E E   E

MA....RY   HAD   A   LIT.....TLE   LAMB,

D D   D   E G   G

LIT.....TLE   LAMB,   LIT.....TLE   LAMB.

E D C D E E   E

MA.....RY   HAD   A   LIT.....TLE   LAMB,

E   D   D   E D   C

ITS   FLEECE   WAS   WHITE   AS   SNOW.

TEACHING SUGGESTIONS:

Ask one child to come up in front of the group to be a lamb and one to be Mary. Discuss what actions and sounds a lamb makes. Then have the two children act out their own scene between Mary and the lamb.

JINGLE BELLS

E E E E E E E
JIN....GLE   BELLS,   JIN....GLE   BELLS

E G C D E
JIN.....GLE   ALL   THE   WAY.

F F F F F E E
OH   WHAT   FUN   IT   IS   TO   RIDE

E E E D D DE DG
IN   A   ONE   HORSE   O....PEN   SLEIGH.

TEACHING SUGGESTIONS:

Get a harness of sleigh bells and ask one child to ring the bells as the rest of the class or group sing the song.

AWAY IN THE MANGER

GGFEE D CC BAG

A....WAY IN A MAN....GER NO CRIB FOR A BED

GGA G GD BA G

THE LIT....TLE LORD JE....SUS LAY DOWN HIS

C E GG FEED

SWEET HEAD THE STARS IN THE SKY

C C B AG

LOOK....ED DOWN WHERE HE LAY,

G FE D ED

THE LIT....TLE LORD JE....SUS

CD ABC

A....SLEEP ON THE HAY.

TEACHING SUGGESTIONS:

To be sung as a Christmas Carol. The Manger Scene can be acted out by the children...need a Mary, Joseph, baby, twinkling star, several animals.

LONDON BRIDGE

GA   G   FE   F   G

LON.....DON   BRIDGE   IS   FALL.....ING   DOWN,

DE   F   E   F   G

FALL.....ING   DOWN,   FALL.....ING   DOWN,

GA   G   FE   F   G

LON.....DON   BRIDGE   IS   FALL.....ING   DOWN

DG   EC

MY   FAIR   LA.....DY.

TEACHING SUGGESTIONS:

1. Ask two children to come to the front of the room. Have them face each other and raise arms to form a bridge. Have the other children walk under the bridge and, on the last word in the song, have the two people lower their arms and catch somebody.
2. You could ask the children what might cause a bridge to fall down. Too heavy a load—badly built bridge—poor materials, etc.

FARMER IN THE DELL

G C CC CC

THE FAR.....MER IN THE DELL

DE EEE E

THE FAR.....MER IN THE DELL

GG A GEC

HI.....HO.. THE DAIR.....Y.....O

DE E DDC

THE FAR.....MER IN THE DELL.

OTHER VERSES:
THE WIFE TAKES THE CHILD
THE CHILD TAKES THE NURSE
THE NURSE TAKES THE DOG
THE DOG TAKES THE CAT
THE CAT TAKES THE RAT
THE RAT TAKES THE CHEESE
THE CHEESE STANDS ALONE

TEACHING SUGGESTIONS:

Have the children form a circle. Choose a farmer and put him in the center of the circle. Have him pick a wife. Then have the wife pick a child and so on all the way through the verses on the opposite page. After the cheese is chosen, have the cheese stand alone in the circle and have the other children who were in the center of the circle return to their old places. The cheese then becomes the new farmer and you begin all over again.

I have done successfully the above with my three-year old group but with the help of an assistant who stayed in the center with the farmer. The age to do the above should be left entirely up to the teacher as only she knows her group's abilities.

THREE BLIND MICE

E D C   E D C

THREE   BLIND   MICE   THREE   BLIND   MICE

G F F E   G F F E

SEE   HOW   THEY   RUN   SEE   HOW   THEY   RUN

G C C B A B C G G

THEY   ALL   RAN   AF....TER   THE   FARM....ER'S   WIFE

G C C C B A B C G

WHO   CUT   OFF   THEIR   TAILS   WITH   A   CARV....ING

G   G G C C B A B

KNIFE   DID   YOU   EV....ER   SEE   SUCH   A

C G G G F E D C

SIGHT   IN   YOUR   LIFE   AS   THREE   BLIND   MICE?

TEACHING SUGGESTIONS:

If you really feel brave and don't mind noise and confusion, you may have the children act out this song. You will need: Blind Mouse 1; Blind Mouse 2; Blind Mouse 3; The Farmer's Wife.
Good Luck!

TWINKLE TWINKLE LITTLE STAR

CC GG AA G

TWIN.....KLE   TWIN.....KLE   LIT.....TLE   STAR

F FE E D D C

HOW   I   WON.....DER   WHERE   YOU   ARE

GGF FEED

UP   A.....BOVE   THE   SKY   SO   HIGH,

GGF FEED

LIKE   A   DIA.....MOND   IN   THE   SKY

CC GG AA G

TWIN.....KLE   TWIN.....KLE   LIT.....TLE   STAR,

F FE E D D C

HOW   I   WON.....DER   WHERE   YOU   ARE.

TEACHING SUGGESTIONS:

Have all of the children stand up and twinkle like a star...some might shake, fall down like a fall star, etc.
This song can be used to introduce a discussion about stars and the Solar System.
Many teachers may decide to just sing this song for fun!

GOOD NIGHT, LADIES

E C G C   E C D D

GOOD   NIGHT,   LA....DIES   GOOD   NIGHT   LA....DIES

E C F F F E E D D C

GOOD   NIGHT   LA....DIES   WE   HATE   TO   SEE   YOU   GO

E D C D E   E E   D D D

MER....RI....LY   WE   ROLL   A....LONG   ROLL   A....LONG

E G G   E D C D E   E E

ROLL   A....LONG   MER....RI....LY   WE   ROLL   A....LONG

D D E D C

O....ER   THE   DEEP   BLUE   SEA.

ALOUETTE

GABB AG ABGD

A....LOU....ET....TE, GEN....TLE A....LOU....ET....TE

GABB AGABG

A....LOU....ET....TE,   JE   TE   PLU....ME....RAI

GGGB DDD

JE   TE   PLU....ME....RAI....LA....TETE,

DEDC BAG

JE   TE   PLU....ME   RAI....LA   TETE

DDD   DDD

ET LA   TETE   ET LA   TETE

D

OH! (begin again)

TEACHING SUGGESTIONS:

I suggest you sing this French song just for fun unless you have someone in the room who knows French well and can provide some enrichment.

DOWN IN THE VALLEY

G C D E C E D C D

DOWN IN THE VAL....LEY,   VAL....LEY SO LOW,

G B D G G   F E

HANG YOUR HEAD O....VER,   HEAR THE

D C G C D E C

WIND BLOW.   HEAR THE WIND BLOW, DEAR,

E D C D

HEAR THE WIND BLOW,

G B D G G

HANG YOUR HEAD O....VER,

F E D C

HEAR THE WIND BLOW!

TEACHING SUGGESTIONS:

Have several or all students stand up and wave their arms as if they were a tree whose leaves are blowing.

FOR HE'S A JOLLY GOOD FELLOW

G E E E D E F E

FOR HE'S A JOL....LY GOOD FEL....LOW

E D D D C D E C

FOR HE'S A JOL....LY GOOD FEL....LOW

C E E E D E F A

FOR HE'S A JOL....LY GOOD FEL....LOW

A G G G F D C

WHICH NO....BODY CAN DE....NY.

TEACHING SUGGESTIONS:

Introduce words Jolly and Fellow. Ask who is often called jolly? Santa Claus is who. Fellow—another word for person.

HICKORY DICKORY DOCK

E FG F F FD E
HIC.....KOR.....Y DIC.....KOR.....Y DOCK

E E G F D E
THE MOUSE RAN UP THE CLOCK

E E E G
THE CLOCK STRUCK ONE

G F F A
THE MOUSE RAN DOWN

G A G F E D C
HIC.....KOR.....Y DIC.....KOR.....Y DOCK.

TEACHING SUGGESTIONS:

1. Have a child find something in the room to represent a clock such as a block of some sort, etc. Then have him find a small object to represent a mouse. (This also could be done by using one's fingers.) As the other children sing the song, allow the child to act it out in his own way. This helps with the understanding of up and down concepts.

I recommend this idea be used no earlier than Kindergarten!

O BEAUTIFUL FOR SPACIOUS SKIES

G G E E G G D D

O BEAU...TI...FUL FOR SPA....CIOUS SKIES,

E F G A B G

FOR AM....BER WAVES OF GRAIN,

G G E E G G D D

FOR PUR....PLE MOUN....TAINS MAJ....ES....TIES

D D D E A D

A....BOVE THE FRUIT....ED PLAIN!

G E E D C C B B

A.....MER.....I.....CA! A.....MER.....I.....CA!

C D B A G C

GOD SHED HIS GRACE ON THEE,

C C A A C C G G

AND CROWN THY GOOD WITH BROTH...ER....HOOD

G A CG DC

FROM SEA TO SHIN....ING SEA!

TEACHING SUGGESTIONS:

A patriotic tune. Discuss what **America** means to each student.

POP GOES THE WEASEL

CCD DE GE C
ALL   A.....ROUND   THE   COB.....BL.....ER'S   BENCH

G CC D DE C
THE   MON...KEY   CHASE.....D   THE   WEA.....SEL

G CC D DEGEC
THE   MON.....KEY   THOUGHT   T'...WAS   ALL   IN   FUN

A D F EC
POP   GOES   THE   WEA.....SEL.

TEACHING SUGGESTIONS:
Choose a child to be the cobbler, the monkey and the weasel. Before the children act out the song, be sure they understand: 1. a cobbler—a mender of shoes; 2. a monkey—an animal many of the children see at the zoo; 3. a weasel—a four legged animal looking a little like a leopard without his spots.
Let the three children chosen act out a short skit about this song.
I suggest the above be used with second and third graders only! No younger!

YANKEE DOODLE

CC DE CE D GCC
YAN....KEE DOO....DLE WENT TO TOWN A RID....ING

DECB G C CD E FE
ON A PO....NY. HE STUCK A FEA....THER IN HIS

D C B GA BCC
HAT AND CALL....ED IT MA....CAR....RONI.

AB A G A BC G A
YAN....KEE DOO....DLE KEEP IT UP YAN....KEE

G FE G A B AG A
DOO....DLE DAN....DY. ALL THE LASS....ES ARE

BC A G CBD CC
SO SWEET. AS SWEET AS SU....GAR CAN....DY.

TEACHING SUGGESTIONS:

Helpful facts: (For 2nd and 3rd graders mainly)
1. This was a favorite song with the Americans in the war they fought against the British in 1775. (Revolutionary War)
2. This is a popular song with those people who live north of the Mason-Dixon line or consider themselves northerners.

THE FIRST NOEL

E D C D E F G

THE.... FIR....ST NO....E....L,

A B C B A G

THE AN....GELS DID SAY

A B C B A G A

WAS TO CER....TAIN POOR SHEP....HERDS

B C G F E E D C D

IN FIELDS AS THEY LAY IN.... FIELDS

E F G A B C B A G

AS THEY LAY KEEP....ING THEIR SHEEP

A B C B A G A

ON A COLD WIN....TERS' NIGHT

B CG FE
THAT   WAS   SO   DEEP

EDCD EFG
NO....   EL,   NO....   EL,

CBA AG
NO....   EL,   NO....EL,

C BAGABCGFE
BORN   IS   THE   KING   OF   IS....   RAE....EL!

TEACHING SUGGESTIONS:

To be sung solely as a Christmas Carol.

OLD MacDONALD HAD A FARM

F F F C D D C

OLD Mac....DON....ALD HAD A FARM

A A G G F

E.... I.... E....I.... O

C F F F

AND ON THIS FARM

C D D C

HE HAD SOME CHICKS

A A G G F

E.... I.... E.... I....O

C C F F F

WITH A CHICK CHICK HERE

C C F F F

AND A CHICK CHICK THERE

F F F F F F

HERE A CHICK THERE A CHICK

FF F FF F

EV....ERY....WHERE   A   CHICK   CHICK

F F FC DDC

OLD   Mac....DON....ALD   HAD   A   FARM

AAGGF

E....   I....   E....   I....O.

TEACHING SUGGESTIONS:

Before you sing: (for 1st-3rd grades)
1. Ask individual children to name the vowels: A, E, I, O, U and sometimes Y.
2. Ask the sound that the long vowels make. They all say their own name.
While singing:
1. Ask children to listen to the words and see if they hear any vowel sounds....answer is E, I and O.
2. Ask children what vowels are missing in the song? Answer is A, U and Y.

SILENT NIGHT

GAG **E** **GAG** **E**

SI.... LENT NIGHT, HO..... LY NIGHT,

DD B **C C G**

ALL IS CALM, ALL IS BRIGHT

A ACBA GA G E

'ROUND YON VIR... GIN MOTH..ER AND CHILD,

AA CBA GA G E

HO...LY INFANT SO TEN...DER AND MILD,

D D FDB CE

SLEEP IN HEAV...EN...LY PEACE

C GE GFD C

SLEEP IN HEAV...EN...LY PEACE.

TEACHING SUGGESTIONS:

This song is sung around Christmas time and can be sung for fun or used in some type of Christmas program.

ROW, ROW YOUR BOAT

C C C D E

ROW   ROW   ROW   YOUR   BOAT

E   DE   F G

GENT.....LY   DOWN   THE   STREAM

CCCGGG

MER.....RI.....LY   MER.....RI.....LY

E EE   CCC

MER.....RI.....LY   MER.....RI.....LY

G FE DC

LIFE   IS   BUT   A   DREAM.

TEACHING SUGGESTIONS:

Ask if anyone has ever been in a boat before? If so what kind of a boat was it? Have child come up and show how he would row a boat.

This is a perfect song to add to a Transportation Unit or Boat Unit—motorboats, sailboats, canoes, rowboats, etc.
I suggest the above activities for the First through Third grade.

TEN LITTLE INDIANS

C C C   C C C   E   GG
ONE   LIT....TLE,   TWO   LIT....TLE,   THREE   LIT....TLE

E D C   D   DD   D   DD
IN....DI....ANS,   FOUR   LIT....TLE   FIVE   LIT....TLE

B DD BAG   CCCC
SIX   LIT....TLE,   IN....DI....ANS,   SEVEN   LIT....TLE

C   CC   E   GG EDC
EIGHT   LIT....TLE,   NINE   LIT....TLE   IN....DI....ANS,

D   DD GGGC
TEN   LIT....TLE,   IN....DI....AN   BOYS....

Second Verse:
Ten little, nine little, eight little Indians, Seven little six little, five little, Indians, Four little, three little two little Indians, One little, Indian boy.

TEACHING SUGGESTIONS:
Before You Sing the Song:
1. Discuss number concepts 1 through 10. In doing this, it is often helpful to show counting by using concrete things such as blocks, fingers, or other items you might have in the room.
2. Single out children who seem to understand number concepts and ask them to come to the front of the room and count up to ten with chosen items. This is good drill for them and also helpful in learning lit appear before a group.

OH! SUSANNA

CD E G GGAGE C D

I..... CAME TO AL....A.....BA.....MA WITH MY

EE DC D CD E G

BAN.....JO ON MY KNEE AND I'M GOING TO

G AGECDE E DDC

LOUI.....SI.....AN.....A MY TRUE LO.....VE FOR TO SEE

F FA A A G G E C

OH! SU.....SAN.....NA, OH DON'T YOU CRY FOR

D CD E G GAGE

ME, I.....'VE COME FROM AL....A.....BA.....MA

CE E DDC

MY BAN.....JO ON MY KNEE.

TEACHING SUGGESTIONS:

Discuss before singing:
1. Location of Alabama—Louisiana (show on map if you can).
2. Discuss what a banjo is...discuss how popular it was especially in the south.

SHE'LL BE COMIN' ROUND THE MOUNTAIN

C D F F F FD C

SHE'LL BE COM....IN' ROUND THE MOUN....TAIN

A C F F GAAA

WHEN SHE COMES.   SHE'LL BE COM....IN' ROUND

A CA G F G CC

THE MOUN....TAIN   WHEN SHE COMES   SHE'LL BE

AA A AG F F F

COM....IN' ROUND THE MOUN....TAIN   SHE'LL BE

DD D DG F E D

COM....IN' ROUND THE MOUN....TAIN   SHE'LL BE

CCC CA G D E F

COM....IN' ROUND THE MOUN....TAIN WHEN SHE COMES

TEACHING SUGGESTIONS:

Pick a child to be an engine, a box car, and a caboose. Have them hold both hands around the other child's waist in front of them and pretend to be a moving train as the class sings.

JOY TO THE WORLD

C B A   **G**   **F E D C**

JOY   TO   THE   WORLD   THE   LORD   IS   COME,

G A   **A B**   **B C**

LET   EARTH   RE....CEIVE   HER   KING;

C C B A G G F E   **C C B**

LET   EV....   'RY   HEART   PRE....PARE

A G G F E   **E**   **E**   **E E E F**

HIM   ROOM,   AND   HEAV'N   AND   NA....TURE

G F E   **D**   **D D D E F**

SING,   AND   HEA....VEN   AND   NATURE   SING

E D C C A G F E F E D C

AND   HEAVEN   AND   HEA....VEN   AND   NATURE   SING.

TEACHING SUGGESTIONS:

     To be sung solely as a Christmas Carol.

BAA BAA BLACK SHEEP

C C G G A A A A
BAA BAA BLACK SHEEP HAVE YOU AN.....Y

G FF EE D D
WOOL? YES SIR, YES SIR, THREE BAGS

C CC CG GG A
FULL. ONE FOR MY MAS.....TER AND ONE

AA G G F F F
FOR MY DAME BUT NONE FOR THE

E EE
NAUGH.....TY BOY

E D D D C
THAT CRIES IN THE LANE.

TEACHING SUGGESTIONS:

A singing nursery rhyme.

AULD LANG SYNE

C   F E F   A G FG

SHOULD   OLD   AC...QUAIN....TANCE   BE   FOR....GOT

AGF F   F   A   CD   D C

AND   NEV....ER   BROUGHT   TO   MIND   SHOULD   OLD

AA   F   G F G   AGF D

AC..QUAIN..TANCE   BE   FOR....GOT   FOR   DAYS   OF

D   C   F   D CAAFGF

AULD   LANG   SYNE   FOR   AULD   LANG   SYNE   MY

G   DCAACD   D C CAA

DEAR   FOR   AULD   LANG   SYNE   WE'LL   TAKE   THE   CUP

FG   FG   AGFDDCF

OF   KIND.....NESS   DEAR   FOR   AULD   LANG   SYNE.

TEACHING SUGGESTIONS:

A song to be sung around the new year.

DIXIE

GEC CCDEF GG
I.....   WISH   I   WER.....E   IN   THE   LAND   OF

GE AA AGA
COT.....TON   OLD   TIMES   THERE   ARE   NOT

GA B CDE C
FOR.....GOT.....TEN,   LOOK   A.....WAY!   LOOK

GC G EG DE C
A.....WAY!   LOOK   A.....WAY!   DIX.....IE   LAND.

GECCCDE FGG G
IN.....   DIX.....   IE   LAN.....D   WHE...RE   I   WAS   BORN

EA AAG AG A B
IN,   EAR.....LY   ON   ONE   FROST.....Y   MOR ..... N,

C DE C GC G EG

LOOK A.....WAY! LOOK A.....WAY! LOOK A.....WAY!

DE C CFAG F DF

DIX.....IE LAND. I WISH I WERE IN DIX.....IE,

DG DG CFA G F

HOO.....RAY! HOO.....RAY! IN DIX.....IE LAND I'LL

DE F DC A FAAG

TAKE MY STAND TO LIVE AND DIE IN DIX.....IE,

AFAGDC A A FGF

A.....WAY! A.....WAY! A.....WAY DOWN SOUTH IN DIXIE,

AFAGDC A A FGF

A.....WAY! A.....WAY! A.....WAY DOWN SOUTH IN DIX.....IE.

TEACHING SUGGESTIONS:
For Second and Third Grades
1. This became a patriotic song of the Confederate States during the Civil War. These were the states that stayed with the south during the war.
2. The song was written by Daniel Emmett in 1859.

O COME, ALL YE FAITHFUL

C C G C D G

OH COME ALL YE FAITH....FUL,

E D E FE D

JOY....FUL AND TRI....UM....PHANT,

C C BAB C D

OH COME YE,   O   CO....ME YE,

E BAGG

TO BE....ETH....LE....HEM,

G FE F E

COME AND BE....HOLD HIM

D EC D BAG

BORN THE KING OF   AN....   GELS,

CC BCDCG

O   COME, LET US   A....DORE HIM,

EE DEFE D

O COME, LET US A....DORE HIM,

EF EDCBCF

O COME, LET US   A....DORE HIM,

EDCC

CHR....IST THE LORD!

ABOUT THE AUTHOR

Nancy Poffenberger, a Northwestern University graduate, has developed a revolutionary new method for teaching virtually anyone who wants to learn how to play the keyboard. She brings music down to its simplest form – that of A, B, C and eventually advances students into the more traditional instruction. Her method of teaching has been extensively tested from Montessori through the third grade as well as by music therapists for children in special education as well as young gifted children. When tested against other methods her method was found to bring more success and good feeling about music than any other method. Her books have been featured in Parents Magazine, The Gifted Child Magazine – Sphinx and in European articles and she does speaking for TV and educational groups.

Ask your local store for other books...